Sarah Keys Evans

The Power of Quiet Courage

ISBN 978–0–8652–6513–4

Typefaces used in this book are Adobe Jenson, Franklin Gothic, and Parlare.

Cover and interior illustration are by Jermaine "J.P." Powell. See his work at jermainepowell.com, and at Instagram @jpyourlife.

Photo Credits: All photos are courtesy of Sarah Keys Evans except for those on pages 47, 53, and 58 (center), which are courtesy Amy Nathan, with page 53 photos taken by Les Atkins. The photo of Dovey Johnson Roundtree on page 57 is courtesy of the Library of Congress.

Distributed by the University of North Carolina Press.

Printed in Canada.

Contents

Sarah Keys Evans's Family Statement v

Author's Note and Acknowledgments vii

CHAPTER 1 A Different Kind of Battle 1

2 A Different Kind of Hero 3

3 Quiet Courage 16

4 A Plan of Attack 24

5 Never Give Up 33

6 Inspiring Others 43

Timeline 50

Afterword: Courage Spreads 53

Glossary 56

Sources 57

Bibliography 58

Sarah Keys Evans's Family Statement

We are honored that young people everywhere will now have the chance to learn about our Aunt Sarah's quiet strength. Her story was once almost forgotten, but we are so proud that it is finally being shared with the next generation. Before many knew her name, she helped open the doors to freedom for others. We hope readers see that bravery doesn't always look big or loud. Sometimes it looks like a single person, sitting quietly, refusing to move. Her legacy demonstrates that everyday people who oppose injustice can also be agents of change.

Alexis Hargrave, *Great Niece of Sarah Keys Evans*

NG THE CIRCLE
Mrs. Sarah Louise Keys Evans
CLO
Sara wearing her Women's
Arm (WAC) Uniform -1952

Author's Note and Acknowledgments

I first learned about Sarah Keys Evans in 2001 when I saw a plaque about her at the Military Women's Memorial, located at the entrance to Arlington National Cemetery. I was a history major in college and had just written a book on women in the military, but had never heard of the victory won by Sarah Keys Evans and Dovey Johnson Roundtree. The Memorial put me in touch with Sarah Keys Evans. I phoned her in January 2004, the first of many conversations we had for nineteen years during our long collaboration and friendship. I was unable to find accounts of her Interstate Commerce Commission (ICC) case in major books on civil rights history, but the Memorial's staff directed me to a 2002 magazine article on Dovey Johnson Roundtree and a 1983 academic book by Catherine Barnes, a graduate student at Columbia University, which describes the legal aspects of the ICC victory (see Bibliography).

Sarah Keys Evans and I collaborated on creating a slim, self-published book about her for young children in 2006, *Take a Seat—Make a Stand*. Three years later, Dovey Johnson Roundtree published a book that describes the legal arguments used in the ICC case. Over the years, Mrs. Evans shared more details with me about her life and I mentioned her in other books I wrote on civil rights history. We both helped the Roanoke Rapids educators in their efforts to install a monument honoring her in 2020.

This new book you're reading now provides a more full account for young readers about her quest for justice than the one from 2006 and also describes something we never imagined was possible when we first met—that Roanoke Rapids would honor her with a monument. This book would not have been possible without the constant support and encouragement of Sarah Keys Evans, who also partnered with me again in creating another book we hope will appear soon for adult readers from Duke University Press.

Also helping with this book for young readers are members of her family—Cornelia Keys Hargrave, John Hargrave, Krys Hargrave, Alexis Hargrave, Leesa Payton Jones, Sonya Keys, Michelle McComb, Joan Dudley, Julie Ann Waters Graves, and Rodney Waters—as well as her supporters in Roanoke Rapids, Rodney Pierce, Rev. Dr. Charles C. McCollum, Sr., Dr. Ervin Griffin, Sr., Ophelia Gould-Faison, and Dr. Georgette Kimball. Helpful also were the staff at the Military Women's Memorial: Judith Bellafaire, Marilla J. Cushman, Britta Granrud, and Brigadier General Wilma L. Vaught, USAF (ret.). Thanks also go to Stephen Farrell of the Brown Library in Washington, North Carolina, and to Sr. Beth Pearson, Archivist of the Sisters, Servants of the Immaculate Heart of Mary, Scranton, PA.

I'm also grateful for Ansley Herring Wegner's help and guidance. In 2023, as soon as she became the Supervisor of the North Carolina Historical Research and Publications Office, she immediately saw the importance of sharing this story with young people; she has carefully shepherded it along its way. Also important has been the support of her supervisor, Dr. Darin Jerome Waters, and the wonderful illustrations by artist Jermaine Powell and careful design work by Sheilah Barrett Carroll. This book's biggest cheerleader has been my husband. Thank you, Carl, for your unwavering encouragement.

Sarah Keys Evans (*center*) with two friends during Basic Training.

1

A Different Kind of Battle

Sarah isn't the kind of person anyone would think would spend a night in jail—or change the world. She was shy as a child. Of all her sisters and brothers, Sarah was the one who would never do anything to cause trouble.

But trouble came Sarah's way on a hot summer night in 1952, at a lonely bus station in North Carolina. Her bus trip had started many hours earlier in New Jersey. She was twenty-three years old then, working at a United States Army hospital in New Jersey. This was her first trip home to North Carolina since joining the Army a year before. How proud her family would be to see her as Private First Class Sarah Louise Keys.

She was sad that two of her brothers wouldn't be there. They were in Korea where U.S. soldiers were fighting in a war. One brother was in the Army. The other was in the Air Force. Women weren't allowed to fight in wartime battles yet. Sarah joined the Army to help in other ways. At the Army hospital in New Jersey, she helped soldiers injured in the war and their families.

But Sarah found herself in a big battle—at that bus station. It wasn't the kind of battle her brothers were fighting. But it was dangerous. Her only weapon was her courage.

Her bravery that night helped her country in a way she never thought was possible. One general has named her "the Army's Rosa Parks." For a long time, few people knew what she did. But now, many remember because of a new monument that honors her. It's near where she faced danger on that night so long ago.

Read on to see how the small-town girl she once was—Sarah Louise Keys—grew up to be what that new monument calls her: a "Trailblazer for Justice."

Her bravery that night helped her country in a way she never thought was possible. One general has named her "the Army's Rosa Parks."

Private First Class Sarah Keys.

2

A Different Kind of Hero

All her life, Sarah was a quiet, thoughtful person—and a hard worker, too. She grew up on a farm in the small town of Washington, North Carolina. Her father, David Keys, was often away. He looked for construction jobs he could do in other cities and states to earn extra money to keep the farm going.

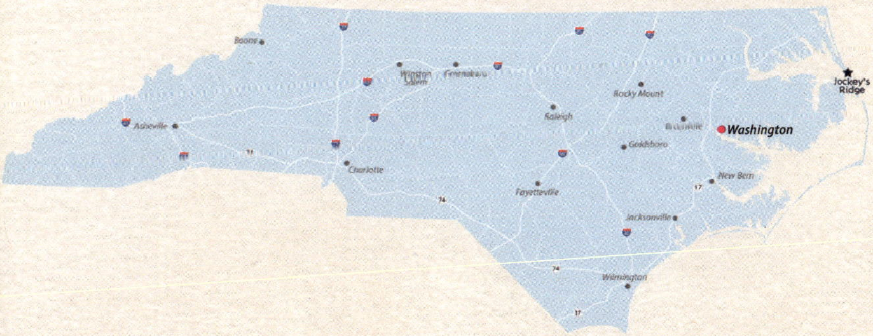

While he was away, Sarah helped her mother, Curley Vivian Keys, run the farm. Sarah liked doing farm chores that got her out of the house, such as milking their cow named Betsy.

There weren't many kids her age near the farm. After finishing her chores, Sarah practiced piano. When she joined her school's band, she practiced French horn, too.

Sometimes she played her horn in the barn, along with one of her brothers, who played trumpet.

She also had fun with her sisters. She loved to fix their hair. She learned how by watching the hairdresser at a beauty shop in town. On special occasions, Sarah and her sisters went to that shop to get their hair done. Sarah would sit by the window and watch what the hair stylist did to fix other people's hair. When it was Sarah's turn to

have her own hair done, she would say, "That's OK. You can take someone else." Sarah just wanted to keep watching what the hairdresser did. Later on, Sarah began to use those ideas to fix her sisters' hair at home. She made up her own creations, too.

Sarah also loved sitting with her father on Sunday afternoons and hearing him tell stories. He told about the little caves on their farmland. Many years ago, there was slavery in North Carolina. Enslaved people had to work on big plantations. They didn't get paid for the work they did. They had no rights and were often treated badly.

Some escaped and hid in the caves on the farm where Sarah would live almost a hundred years later. Free Black men who weren't enslaved owned the farm back when there was slavery. They could have been arrested for letting freedom-seekers hide in those caves. They took that risk because it was the right thing to do.

Her father also told Sarah how he went north as a teenager to live in the other Washington—the nation's capital, Washington, D. C. It was three hundred miles away. He wasn't escaping from slavery. It had ended many years before. Instead, there was segregation in North Carolina—laws and rules that kept people apart because of the color of their skin.

Because of segregation, Black people couldn't go to the same schools as white people, or to the same libraries, parks, restaurants, or the same hospitals. His town's schools for Black students weren't as good as the ones for White students. Segregation also made it hard for Black workers to find good-paying jobs.

When he was a teen, Sarah's father heard from a friend that there were good-paying jobs in Washington, D. C. That city also had a very good high school for Black students. So he moved there on his own. He lived there with friends for a few years and went to that high school. Then, he joined the Navy.

When he moved back to his hometown of Washington, North Carolina, he bought a farm. Soon he helped the Catholic Church start a very good school for Black children right there in his own hometown, the Mother of Mercy School. It opened in 1927, two years before Sarah was born.

This school gave Sarah such a good education that she didn't mind walking an hour in the morning to get there—and another hour to get back home in the afternoon. The school was three miles from her family's farm. There were no school buses back then for students who went to a Catholic school. Sarah's father had a truck, but he needed it for farm work. So Sarah and her brothers and sisters became good walkers.

All that walking was worth it because the school had many extras that other schools back then didn't have. It taught students to sing and play instruments. It had a science lab and a good library. The school also put on plays and concerts. On holidays, the school showed movies. Everyone sat together to watch those movies. That didn't happen in the town's movie theater. That movie theater made Black people sit up in the balcony. White people sat in the better seats downstairs. Sarah's school didn't have segregation rules like that for its movies—or for its concerts and performances, either.

Sarah loved her family. She loved the farm and the school her father helped start. But she had learned from her father's stories that there was no future for her in her hometown. There was segregation and not many really good jobs for Black people in that town.

After graduating from high school in 1948, Sarah moved north to New Jersey. Her older sister had moved there a few years before. She sent Sarah a bus ticket to use to join her there. Some extra jobs her father did were in New Jersey. It seemed like a good place to go to start a new life.

For a while, Sarah went to school in New Jersey. Then she saw an ad for the Women's Army Corps. It talked about seeing the world and being trained for jobs. There wasn't segregation in the Army. Soldiers—Black and White—worked together. In 1951, she signed up to join the Army. Becoming a member of the Women's Army Corps gave her more self confidence.

Before Sarah left home, her father told her one more story—about new rules for bus rides. Some southern states had segregation laws that made Black people sit in the back of a bus. Northern states like New Jersey didn't have laws like that. If a bus trip started in New Jersey, Black riders could sit anywhere. But when the bus drove into a state with segregation, Black riders had to get up and move to the back of the bus.

In 1946, the U. S. Supreme Court tried to stop all that seat-changing. It said that on a trip that went from one state to another state, Black passengers didn't have to move to a new seat when the bus drove into a state with segregation laws.

Because of that court case, Sarah thought she could sit anywhere on a bus. She had taken a few bus trips home before joining the Army. Those trips went well. Her 1952 trip changed her life.

3

Quiet Courage

On Friday morning, August 1, 1952, Sarah started her bus trip home from New Jersey. Dressed in her Army uniform, she chose a seat in the middle of the bus. That's where she sat on her earlier trips home, too. She fell asleep as the bus rolled through New Jersey, Pennsylvania, Maryland, Washington, D.C., and Virginia.

Just after midnight, the bus made its first stop in North Carolina, in the small city of Roanoke Rapids. It would be a few more hours before the bus reached her hometown. A new driver—a tall White man—took charge of the bus. He walked down the aisle, collecting a ticket stub from everyone. When he got to Sarah, he told her to move to the back of the bus.

She was just waking up and was still a little sleepy. She knew she had a long way to go before reaching her hometown. She told the driver that she was comfortable where she was sitting. She had no idea that something dangerous was about to happen.

The driver took the ticket from the White soldier sitting next to Sarah. Then the driver collected tickets from other riders. When he passed by her seat again, Sarah reached out to give him her ticket. He wouldn't take it.

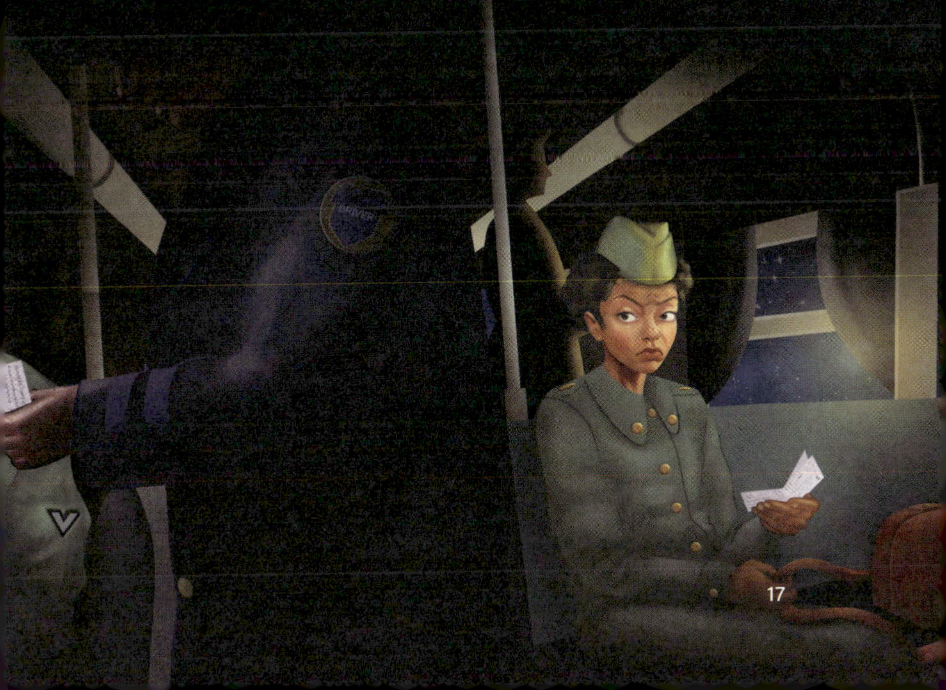

The driver told everyone to get off the bus and get on another bus. He said the woman who wouldn't move her seat had to stay on the bus. But it wasn't going anywhere that night.

Sarah was surprised and a little worried. How could she stay on the bus all night by herself?

The other passengers lined up outside to get on a new bus. So did Sarah. But the driver didn't let her on the new bus.

Sarah walked into the bus station. Maybe there was something wrong with her ticket. The White woman selling tickets wouldn't talk to Sarah. A tall Black man was in the bus station, too. He was cleaning up, pushing a broom. He told Sarah, "Miss, don't you know where you are?"

Suddenly, Sarah felt scared. She knew bad things could happen to Black people who were all alone at night in a small southern town. She walked back outside. Two White police officers came up on either side of her. One put his hand on her shoulder. He led her to a police car. She was so afraid, she didn't try to get away.

They put her into the police car and started driving down a long, dark road.

"Where are you taking me?" Sarah asked.

"We're taking you to jail," one officer said.

"Why?" asked Sarah.

"We can get you for anything. For disorderly conduct," he said. "We don't really even have to get you to jail." When he said that, Sarah got really scared.

She was afraid they might hurt her. She had heard of that happening to other Black people. She stayed very quiet. She listened carefully to everything they said. She was trying to figure out what was happening.

Soon they reached the police station. The officers took her to see the chief of police. He said he was going to lock her up in jail for disorderly conduct.

Sarah knew that people who are put in jail have the right to make one phone call. She asked if she could call her grandparents. Her parents didn't have a phone. The officer said he would phone them for her. Sarah gave him their phone number. He pretended to call. Sarah learned later that her grandparents never got a call.

The police took her to a jail cell. There was a mattress on the floor. It was so dirty Sarah wouldn't touch it. She was all alone. There was nobody to help her. Nobody to talk to. She stayed awake all night. She kept walking back and forth in that jail cell. Walking, and crying, and praying.

The next morning, Saturday morning, the jailer took her to see the chief of police again. He asked her, "What kind of outfit is that you're wearing?"

Sarah said she was in the United States Army, wearing the uniform of the Women's Army Corps.

It was daylight. She wasn't as afraid as she was the night before. So, she added, "You mean you didn't know the color of the Army uniform?"

That made the police chief angry.

He said that's why she spent the night in jail "because you're too damn smart." He said she might get her face slapped.

Sarah knew that some White people didn't like it when Black people did well. Seeing her in that Army uniform seemed to upset the police chief.

Then he said Sarah could go if she paid him $25. That would be like asking for $200 today. Luckily she had enough money with her to pay him.

Policemen then took her to a new bus that was going to her hometown. They forced her to sit in the back. She stayed there. Sarah wanted to get out of that town before something worse happened.

The bus made so many stops that it didn't reach her hometown until Sunday morning. She was a whole day late getting home.

There was no way to phone her family to say what bus she was on. There were no cellphones back then. She took a taxi to get to her family's home. Sarah knew her parents would be very worried.

4

A Plan of Attack

When Sarah got home, she told her father what had happened. He was very angry. Not with Sarah. He was angry with the police.

She told her father that the police arrested her for being "disorderly." But she explained that she wasn't disorderly at all. She hadn't shouted or yelled or done anything like that.

Her father said he knew she hadn't been disorderly. That was a word police sometimes used when they wanted to arrest someone but didn't have anything else to arrest them for.

Her father wanted to help Sarah prove that the police had no right to arrest her. He also had a bigger goal—to put an end to all segregation. Sarah was with him all the way.

They drove to the city of Roanoke Rapids where Sarah had been arrested to try to get officials there to drop the arrest charges. That didn't work.

So her father phoned friends in Washington, D. C.

They told him about Dovey Johnson Roundtree, a young woman lawyer who had been born in North Carolina. She had just finished going to law school in Washington, D. C. At that law school, she had met civil rights lawyers who were getting ready for a big court case that they hoped would end segregation in schools.

Sarah's father phoned this lawyer. Would she want to help end segregation on buses, too? Yes, indeed!

Sarah and her father traveled to Washington, D.C., to talk with this lawyer.

At first, Sarah felt shy. She had never met a lawyer before. She felt more comfortable when she heard that Dovey Johnson Roundtree used to be in the Women's Army Corps, too. They also had something else in common. This young lawyer had been treated very unfairly on a bus ride while she was in the Army. They both wanted to find a way to stop that from happening to others.

What about the 1946 Supreme Court case that Sarah's father told her about? The one that said Black people traveling from one state to another state could sit anywhere on a bus? Sarah and her father learned that this 1946 Supreme Court decision had a "loophole."

That loophole let bus companies do whatever they wanted. This 1946 case was called *Morgan v. Virginia.* It started when a young Black woman, Irene Morgan, was taking a bus from Virginia to go first to Washington, D. C., and then on to Maryland where she lived. Virginia had a segregation law that said Black riders couldn't sit next to White riders. But Washington, D. C., didn't have laws like that. It let Black riders sit anywhere. While the bus was in Virginia, its segregation law made Irene give up her seat to a White rider and then have to stand up for the rest of the trip. Irene protested and was arrested.

The Supreme Court decided that what happened to Irene wasn't fair because the bus was heading to Washington where she could have sat anywhere. So the court said that on state-to-state bus trips, one state can't force people to obey its segregation "law" because there needs to be one plan for seating that would be the same for the whole trip.

But—and here comes the "loophole"—the Court didn't say that "rules" a bus company makes are also forbidden. It said only that a state seating "law" can't be used. So southern bus companies just made their own rules that made Black passengers sit in the back. Not all bus drivers used those rules. But the bus driver in Roanoke Rapids did.

Sarah and her lawyer set out to put an end to this loophole. That might take a long time. Sarah's father said if she ever wanted to stop, she could. But Sarah said as long as her father was there to help her, she would never give up. She knew she had been treated unfairly. It was unfair to be put in jail for being disorderly when she wasn't disorderly.

She was ready to speak up because it was the right thing to do. She wanted to keep that from happening to anyone else.

After meeting with the lawyer, Sarah returned to her job at the Army hospital in New Jersey. She told her two best friends in the Army what had happened. One was Black and the other was White. Both were so sorry that Sarah had been arrested. Sarah also told her commanding officer. But she didn't tell anyone else. Being arrested had upset her. She thought she had to be more careful about everything she said and did. She didn't want anything else bad to happen.

Her lawyer tried to file a complaint in court. That didn't go well. Then her lawyer tried the government office that is in charge of bus travel: the Interstate Commerce Commission, also called the "ICC." On September 1, 1953, her lawyer filed a complaint at the ICC for Sarah that asked the ICC to do something about how unfairly Sarah had been treated. The complaint was named *Sarah Keys v. Carolina Coach Company*. The "*v.*" stands for the Latin word "versus," which means against.

The next month, Sarah's two-year tour of duty in the Army ended. She didn't join up again. She wanted to do something new. The Army gives soldiers money to go to school after leaving the Army. Sarah used her money to do something she had loved doing ever since she was a little girl. She went to beauty school in New York City to become a hair stylist.

The next spring, Dovey Roundtree asked Sarah to come to Washington, D.C., to tell the story of her arrest to

members of the ICC. At first, Sarah was afraid to do this. But her father said he and her younger brother would be there with her. They would sit in the section for visitors in the ICC's meeting room. Knowing they would be there helped give Sarah the courage to tell her story.

Lawyers for the bus company were there, too. They kept trying to trick Sarah into saying that she had shouted and cursed in Roanoke Rapids. They tried to have her say that someone had made her take that bus trip so she would get arrested. Sarah stayed calm and polite as she told the truth. Then, she went back to New York to wait for the ICC to make a decision.

Four months later, in September 1954, the ICC sent Dovey Roundtree a letter.

What a shock—Sarah had lost!

The ICC based its decision on a Supreme Court case from more than fifty years earlier. That 1896 Supreme Court decision said that segregation was OK if the separate things for Black people were equal to those for white people. The bus company lawyer said that a seat in the back of the bus was as good as the seat where Sarah was sitting. So the ICC decided that the bus company hadn't treated Sarah badly when it tried to make her to move to the back.

But the ICC forgot that something else wasn't at all equal about Sarah's trip. She was not treated with the same respect and courtesy as the white passengers.

Dovey Roundtree wasn't ready to give up.

Neither was Sarah.

5

Never Give Up

Sarah's lawyer found a way to make the ICC take a second look at Sarah's case. The ICC decision had been written by only one person. That was unfair, said Sarah's lawyer. Sarah's congressman agreed. They persuaded the ICC to have all eleven of the ICC's official members judge Sarah's case.

Her lawyer felt that Sarah had a better chance of winning this time because of a new decision the U. S. Supreme Court had just made. In 1954, this court said that segregation in schools was unfair and had to end. Dovey Roundtree explained to the ICC that if segregation was unfair for schools, it should be unfair for bus trips, too.

Finally, on Friday morning November 25, 1955—the day after Thanksgiving—Sarah got the phone call she had been waiting for.

Finally, on Friday morning November 25, 1955—the day afterThanksgiving—Sarah got the phone call she had been waiting for. She was working at a New York City beauty shop. Dovey Roundtree phoned to say that the ICC had reached a new decision.

This time Sarah won!

The ICC said that segregation had to end on all state-to-state bus trips, no matter what laws a state had or what rules a bus company had. Not only that, on the same day, the ICC said that segregation had to end on all train trips, too.

Sarah shared the news with everyone in the beauty shop. They were shocked that their quiet friend was helping to end segregation. Before then, Sarah had been afraid to talk with them about her arrest. She didn't know if they would want to work with someone who had been arrested.

Now, she was talking about her arrest and ICC victory with people at the beauty shop and also with newspaper and TV reporters who came there to learn more. The next day, newspapers across the country reported on the brave young woman who stood up for her rights and the rights of all people of color.

However, her ICC victory didn't end segregation on a different kind of bus trip—on local bus rides that didn't go into another state. One week after Sarah's victory was announced, another brave woman stepped up to end segregation on that kind of bus trip. On December 1, 1955, Rosa Parks was arrested for not moving to the back of a local bus in Montgomery, Alabama. Big protests followed, led by Rev. Dr. Martin Luther King, Jr. For a year, Black people in Montgomery refused to ride the local buses until

segregation ended. Finally, in December 1956, the U. S. Supreme Court reached a decision in a case brought by some other Alabama women. The court said that segregation on Montgomery's local city buses had to end.

Even that didn't end segregation everywhere. Most parts of the country obeyed the new rules the ICC wrote in the decision it made in Sarah's case. But many southern states didn't obey those rules. The ICC did nothing to make them obey.

It took hundreds of young people—Black and White—to force bus companies to obey the ICC's Sarah Keys rules. Those young people were called Freedom Riders. On May 4, 1961, they started taking bus rides in southern states where bus stations still had segregation

rules. Many Freedom Riders were arrested and beaten for not obeying the segregation rules. Reports about that in newspapers and on TV around the world made the U. S. government look bad. Finally, it took action.

On May 29, 1961, U. S. Attorney General Robert F. Kennedy, the nation's highest legal official, told the ICC that it must make bus companies obey its rules, including the rules in the *Sarah Keys v. Carolina Coach Company* decision.

This time, the ICC took firm action. Segregation soon ended on buses, trains and on airplanes, too.

Protests against other kinds of segregation continued around the U. S. until Congress passed the Civil Rights Act of 1964. It made segregation illegal in any kind of business that served the public.

The battle against segregation took a long time, with many people stepping up to help win the fight. One of them was a real soldier, Private First Class Sarah Louise Keys. She said she was glad to "help unlock another door of freedom."

Attorney General Robert F. Kennedy orders the ICC to comply with the *Sarah Keys v. Carolina Coach Company* ruling.

6

Inspiring Others

After her ICC victory, Sarah went back to doing what she loved most—helping women look and feel beautiful by creating hairstyles for them at beauty shops in Brooklyn, New York. Soon she met the man who would be her husband, George Evans. This handsome Texan had come to New York to be a singer. Later, he worked as a counselor for young people. He helped her open her own beauty shop, the Glamour Nook. After their wedding in 1958, she became known as Sarah Keys Evans. She never had children of her own but was close to her many nieces, nephews, and other family members.

Wedding photo of Mr. and Mrs. Evans, 1958.

Many books on civil rights history tell about famous people, such as Rosa Parks, Dr. King, or the Freedom Riders, and their big protests. Most of those books don't mention Sarah's quiet victory. Few remembered what she did until a new museum opened to honor military women. In 1998, that museum—the Military Women's Memorial—put up a sign about Sarah's ICC victory. That's how the author of the book you're reading now first heard about Sarah and got to meet her.

Many books on civil rights history tell about famous people, such as Rosa Parks, Dr. King, or the Freedom Riders, and their big protests. Most of those books don't mention Sarah's quiet victory.

Soon, others heard about her, too, including people in Roanoke Rapids, where she was arrested so many years before. In 2018, Black educators there learned about a contest that would give money to ten North Carolina communities to honor someone who did something important that most people didn't know about. They decided to win that contest for Sarah—and they did!

They had help from some White people in Roanoke Rapids who had come to understand what their Black neighbors always knew: **that segregation was unfair and just plain wrong.**

On Saturday, August 1, 2020—sixty-eight years after Sarah got on the bus that led to her arrest—Roanoke Rapids held a ceremony to dedicate a huge monument that honors her. It sits in the middle of the city's Dr. Martin Luther King, Jr., Park. The monument has paintings on its walls that tell the story of how Sarah helped end segregation. A sign on the monument calls her a "Trailblazer for Justice."

Sarah had just celebrated her 91st birthday. She wasn't able to travel to North Carolina for the ceremony. She was also sad that her husband, parents, and lawyer hadn't lived long enough to see her receive this honor. But Sarah was able to speak by phone with those at the ceremony. She told them how proud and happy she was about all they had done.

Her hometown of Washington, North Carolina, has also honored her. It named a street for her and tells her story in its history museum. There's also a historical marker about her now in Roanoke Rapids. The Military Women's Memorial keeps celebrating her in its exhibits. The U.S. Army mentions her on its website. These exhibits, the monument, and the book you're reading now all show that everyone—even quiet, shy people—can step up and have the courage to help make the world a better place, as Sarah Louise Keys Evans did all those many years ago.

Children viewing art at the Sarah Keys Evans Monument in Roanoke Rapids, NC.

HE CIRCLE
POLICE DEPT.
Sarah Keys is arrested as the Roanoke
apids Bus Station for refusing to move to
back of the bus, NC - Aug. 1 1952
Sarah Keys spent the night in the
Roanoke Rapids Jail.

WINNER ACCLAIMS DECISION BY I. C. C.

Negro Woman in Bus Case Voices Happiness Here at Segregation Ban

DRAWS I.C.C. RULING: Miss Sarah Keys of New York, who sued Carolina Coach Company, a bus line at Raleigh, N. C.

Sarah Keys in a *New York Times* article, Nov. 27, 1955.

Sarah (*right*) with her sister, Cornelia, 1950s.

Timeline

1929 Sarah Louise Keys is born on April 18 in Washington, North Carolina.

1946 *Morgan v. Virginia* U.S. Supreme Court decision says states may not force interstate travelers to obey Jim Crow bus-seating *laws*, but the court says nothing about *rules* a bus company makes.

1948 Sarah graduates from Mother of Mercy High School in Washington, North Carolina.

1951 Sarah enters the U.S. Army's Women's Army Corps (WAC).

1952 On August 2, Sarah is arrested at a bus station in Roanoke Rapids, North Carolina, for not moving to the back of a bus on a trip that started hours earlier in New Jersey.

Sarah and her father meet with lawyer Dovey Johnson Roundtree in Washington, D.C.

1953 In February, the U.S. District Court for the District of Columbia refuses to hear a lawsuit Sarah's lawyer filed against the bus company that had her arrested; the court says it doesn't have jurisdiction.

On September 1, Sarah's lawyer files a complaint called *Sarah Keys v. Carolina Coach Company* at the Interstate Commerce Commission (ICC).

On November 27, Sarah is honorably discharged from the WAC.

1954 On May 12, the ICC holds a hearing on the Sarah Keys case; Sarah testifies.

On May 17, the Supreme Court issues its *Brown v. Board of Education* decision ending school segregation.

On September 30, the ICC rules against Sarah Keys.

On October 19, Sarah's lawyer files a new document at the ICC to have it reconsider her case.

1955 On November 7, the ICC rules in favor of *Sarah Keys v. Carolina Coach Company,* ending discrimination of seating on interstate buses; the ICC reaches a similar decision on trains.

On November 25, the ICC decision is announced to the public.

On December 1, Rosa Parks is arrested in Montgomery, Alabama.

1958 Sarah Keys marries George Evans; her name changes to Sarah Keys Evans.

1961 On May 4, the Freedom Rides begin.

On May 29, Attorney General Robert Kennedy urges the ICC to finally enforce the *Keys* decision.

1997 The Military Women's Memorial opens at the entrance to Arlington National Cemetery.

1998 The Military Women's Memorial puts up a plaque about Sarah Keys Evans and Dovey Roundtree.

2006 Sarah Keys Evans receives the Trailblazer Award from the U.S. Department of Justice.

2010 The Roanoke Rapids Canal Museum puts up a small poster about Sarah Keys Evans.

2019 A committee of Black educators in Roanoke Rapids wins a contest sponsored by the Z. Smith Reynolds Foundation, providing funds to create a monument to honor Sarah Keys Evans.

2020 On August 1, a ceremony is held in Roanoke Rapids, North Carolina, to dedicate a monument honoring Sarah Keys Evans; the monument is in the city's Martin Luther King, Jr. Park.

2022 A historical marker about the Sarah Keys ICC decision is installed in Roanoke Rapids.

2023 Sarah Keys Evans dies, at age 94. Before her death, she knew that this book would be published to inspire others.

Children at Sarah Keys Evans Monument, Roanoke Rapids, N.C.

Afterword: Courage Spreads

Sarah Keys Evans' quiet courage has inspired many others, including the educators in Roanoke Rapids who hope the monument they installed will encourage people to stand up for what's right, as she did. Those educators—Rev. Dr. Charles C. McCollum, Sr., Dr. Ervin Griffin, Sr., Dr. Georgette Kimball, and Ophelia Gould-Faison—learned of Sarah Keys Evans thanks to another educator in that city, Rodney Pierce. He first heard about Sarah Keys Evans in 2011 while working in his city's history museum. The museum's director had come across an old newspaper article about her and posted a sign about her in the museum in 2010. Rodney Pierce then learned of a small self-published children's book about her that Amy Nathan and Sarah Keys Evans wrote in 2006. He contacted them to learn more because he wanted his city to honor her. The Z. Smith Reynolds Foundation's contest provided the perfect opportunity. The monument committee recorded an interview with Sarah Keys Evans in 2019 that can be heard on the monument's website (see Bibliography). The committee also created an award—the Sarah Keys Evans

Trailblazer Award—to honor others who stand up for justice. Rodney Pierce had a historical marker about her ICC victory installed in Roanoke Rapids in 2022.

People in other cities also help people learn about her, including Leesa Jones, founder of the Underground Railroad Museum in Washington, North Carolina. The Military Women's Memorial continues to include Sarah Keys Evans in its exhibits. The U. S. Army features her on its website and the U. S. Department of Justice gave her its Trailblazer Award in 2006. Her sister, Cornelia Keys Hargrave, a retired school teacher, always told her students about her older sister during Black History Month. Another relative, Krys Hargrave, who teaches in New Jersey high schools, often tells students about Sarah Keys Evans and invited her to speak with students at one of those schools in 2017, the Academy for Urban Leadership Charter School in Perth Amboy. Nephew Rodney Waters wrote about his courageous aunt in the *Catholic Review*. Niece Julie Ann Waters Graves has come to the ceremonies dedicating the monument and historical marker to thank everyone for honoring her Aunt Sarah.

Law schools teach students about her 1955 ICC victory because it was the first time the ICC ruled against the segregation policy of "separate-but-equal" that had been endorsed by the U. S. Supreme Court in its 1896 decision

Plessy v. Ferguson. In 1954, the U. S. Supreme Court also ruled against "separate-but-equal" in *Brown v. Board of Education*. A new age of fairness was starting. Sarah Keys Evans helped make that happen.

Sarah Keys Evans, 1948.

Sarah, 1950s.

Glossary

ceremony a formal, public event celebrating something important

disorderly not being peaceful, not obeying the law

enslaved someone who is forced to lose their freedom

Interstate Commerce Commission (ICC) a part of the U.S. government from 1887 to 1996 that supervised business between U.S. states, including bus and train travel

lawyer someone who has studied about laws in law school

legal having to do with laws

loophole a problem in a law that lets someone disobey it

monument a statue or large structure that honors a famous person or event

segregation separating people by skin color, age, religion or other features

slavery forcing people to work without pay or freedom

U.S. Supreme Court the country's highest court

trailblazer a pioneer, someone who makes a new way forward

Women's Army Corps from 1942–1978, the branch of the U.S. Army that women could join; now women can serve in all parts of the Army

Sarah in her Army uniform, 1951.

Dovey Johnson Roundtree, 1940s.

Sources

Quotes from Sarah Keys Evans and personal information about her come from the many conversations she had with Amy Nathan from January 2004 to August 2023. Others who provided information include several of Sarah Keys Evans' relatives—Cornelia Keys Hargrave, Krys Hargrave, Leesa Payton Jones, Sonya Keys, Michelle McComb, Joan Dudley, and Julie Ann Waters Graves—as well as educators in Roanoke Rapids, North Carolina: Dr. Ervin Griffin, Sr., Ophelia Gould-Faison, Dr. Georgette Kimball, Rev. Dr. Charles C. McCollum, Sr., and Rodney Pierce, as well as photographer Les Atkins. Staff members of the Military Women's Memorial provided information on Sarah Keys Evans and the memorial's founder, Air Force Brigadier General Wilma L. Vaught (ret.), called Sarah Keys Evans "the Army's Rosa Parks." Books and articles in the Bibliography provided additional information. The Bibliography also has links to the text of the ICC decision *Sarah Keys v. Carolina Coach Company*, and to a videotaped 2019 interview with Sarah Keys Evans.

Sarah Keys Evans, 2019.

Bibliography

Books

Barnes, Catherine A. *Journey from Jim Crow: The Desegregation of Southern Transit.* New York: Columbia University Press, 1983. See pages 19, 38–40, 44–51, 87–88, 92–94, 96–116, 121–4, 157–189, 197, 205.

Bay, Mia. *Traveling Black: A Story of Race and Resistance.* Cambridge, Massachusetts: Harvard University Press, 2021. See pages 164–165, 191, 230–232, 249–251, 261, 263–267, 269, 270–283.

Crow, Jeffrey J., Paul D. Escott, and Flora J. Hatley Wadelington. *A History of African Americans in North Carolina.* Chapel Hill: North Carolina Office of Archives and History, 2019. See pages 118–141, 165.

Jones, Leesa Payton. *Bright Ma: Day Clean—A Story About the Underground Railroad.* Washington, NC: Book Baby, 2020. See page 5.

Loy, Ursula Fogelman and Pauline Marion Worthy, editors. *Washington and the Pamlico.* Washington-Beaufort County Bicentennial Commission, 1976. See pages 265–267, 302.

McCabe, Katie and Jabari Asim. *Mighty Justice: The Untold Story of Civil Rights Trailblazer Dovey Johnson Roundtree.* New York: Roaring Brook Press, 2020. See pages 99–119.

McWhorter, Diane. *A Dream of Freedom: The Civil Rights Movement from 1954 to 1968.* New York: Scholastic, 2004. See pages 13–65, 107.

Nathan, Amy. *Round and Round Together: Taking a Merry-go-Round Ride into the Civil Rights Movement.* Philadelphia: Paul Dry Book, 2011. See page 93.

Nathan, Amy. *Take a Seat—Make a Stand: A Hero in the Family.* Lincoln, NE: iUniverse, 2006. See pages 5–69.

Nathan, Amy. *Together: An Inspiring Response to the "Separate-but-Equal" Supreme Court Decision that Divided America.* Philadelphia: Paul Dry Books, 2021, 2nd Edition 2023. See pages 59–75, 85–95, 158–159.

Roundtree, Dovey Johnson and Katie McCabe. *Mighty Justice: My Life in Civil Rights.* Chapel Hill: Algonquin Books, 2019; originally published in 2009 by the University Press of Mississippi. See pages 54, 64–67, 96, 102–103, 124–155, 176–179.

Tyner, Artika R. The Untold Story of Sarah Keys Evans: Civil Rights Soldier. Capstone Press, 2023.

Sarah Keys Evans with a plaque about her at the Military Women's Memorial.

Sarah's mother, father, and her brother William, 1950s.

Articles

Bell, T. Anthony. "The quietly defiant, unlikely fighter: Pfc Sarah Keys and the fight for justice and humanity." February 20, 2014. Available on the website of the U.S. Army: https://www.army.mil.

Bellafaire, Judith. "Challenging the System: Two Army Women Fight for Equality." 2002. Women in Military Service For America Memorial Foundation, Inc.

Bowman, Susan. "Sarah Louise Keys: An Unsung Hero in the Fight for Civil Rights." *Our Heritage*, February 2011.

Curtis, Clark. "The Story of Keysville." Washington (N.C.) *Daily News*, February 8, 2023.

Jones, Leesa. "A Town of Grace." Washington (N.C.) *Daily News*, February 9, 2022.

Martin, Lance. "Marker honoring Keys unveiled at site where she was arrested." RRspin.com, January 15, 2022. Available at: https://www.rrspin.com/news/5345-marker-honoring-keys-unveiled-at-site-where-she-was-arrested.html

Martin, Lance. "Saluting Sheer Bravery: Keys-Evans honored." RRspin.com, August 3, 2020. Available at: https://www.rrspin.com/news/3148-saluting-sheer-bravery-keys-evans-honored.html

Martin, Lance. "Trailblazers honored at Keys Evans celebration." RRspin.com, July 31, 2022. Available at: https://www.rrspin.com/news/6225-trailblazers-honored-at-keys-evans-celebration.html

McCabe, Katie. "She Had a Dream." *Washingtonian Magazine*, March 2002.

Price, Jay. "A new focus on the women who helped end discrimination on interstate buses." NPR. November 17, 2021.

Waters, Rodney. "A hero in the family: Sarah made history." *The Catholic Review*, April 24, 2007.

Waxman, Olivia. "Years Before Rosa Parks, Sarah Keys Refused to Give Up Her Seat on a Bus. Now She's Being Honored in the City Where She Was Arrested." TIME.com, July 29, 2020.

Newspaper Articles from 1955 and 1961 about Sarah Keys Evans' ICC Victory

"Great Thing, Says Victor in Bias Cas: Ex-Wac Tells of Bus Episode." *New York Herald Tribune*, November 26, 1955.

Greene, Jerry. "ICC Orders Jim Crow Off Trains, Buses" *New York Daily News*, November 26, 1955.

Huston, Luther. "I.C.C. Orders End of Segregation on Trains, Buses." *New York Times*, November 26, 1955.

"ICC Ruling on Travel 'Frees' Brooklyn Girl. *New York Age, Defender*, December 3, 1955.

Lerner, Max. "We Ride Together." *New York Post*, November 28, 1955.

"Robert Kennedy Asks I.C.C. to End Bus Segregation." *New York Times*, May 30, 1961.

Document

"*Sarah Keys v. Carolina Coach Company*." Text of the ICC decision is available on Amy Nathan's website at: http://www.amynathanbooks.com/attachments/keys.pdf or at: https://babel.hathitrust.org/cgi/pt?id=uc1.b2949044&view=1up&seq=815

Websites

Sarah Keys Evans Monument Project: https://sarahkevansproject.com

Women in Military Service for America Memorial: https://www.womensmemorial.org

Z. Smith Reynolds Foundation Inclusive Public Art Project: https://www.zsr-inclusivepublicart.com

Video and Audio Files

"Black History Month: Local Hero." (A radio interview with Sarah Keys Evans.) The Brian Lehrer Show, WNYC-FM, February 9, 2011. Available at: https://www.wnyc.org/story/113646-black-history-month-local-hero/

"Interview of Sarah Keys Evans." (Video interview with Sarah Keys Evans) Sarah K. Evans Inclusive Public Art Project, March 31, 2019. https://sarahkevansproject.com/who-is-sarah-keys-evans/

About the Illustrator

Jermaine Powell ("JP") is a unique voice within contemporary art. JP is a North Carolina based mixed-media painter, public artist, and a widely recognized luxury art specialist, creating unforgettable visual experiences that fuse bold design with cultural storytelling.

Known for his lush, multidimensional paintings and immersive public installations, JP celebrates art history, community, leadership, nature, and human connection through a lens that is as globally inspired as it is deeply personal. A seasoned world traveler, he incorporates jewelry, collectibles, exotic birds, animals, and luxury materials into his richly textured work, transforming dried florals, vivid patterns, and tactile surfaces into narratives of transformation and identity.

Website: jermainepowell.com
Instagram: @jpyourlife